W9-BSS-058

# WEEKLY WR READER®
## EARLY LEARNING LIBRARY

**Animals That Live in the Mountains/
Animales de las montañas**

# Mountain Goats/
# Cabra montés

by/por JoAnn Early Macken

Reading consultant/Consultora de lectura:
Susan Nations, M.Ed.,
author/literacy coach/consultant in literacy development
autora/tutora de alfabetización/
consultora de desarrollo de la lectura

Please visit our web site at: **www.garethstevens.com**
For a free color catalog describing our list of high-quality books,
call 1-800-542-2595 (USA) or 1-800-387-3178 (Canada).

Library of Congress Cataloging-in-Publication Data

Macken, JoAnn Early, 1953-
   [Mountain goats. Spanish & English]
   Mountain goats = Cabra montés / by JoAnn Early Macken.
     p. cm. — (Animals that live in the mountains = Animales de las montañas)
   Includes bibliographical references and index.
   ISBN 0-8368-6451-4 (lib. bdg.)
   ISBN 0-8368-6458-1 (softcover)
   1. Mountain goat—Juvenile literature.   I. Title: Cabra montés.   II. Title.
  QL737.U53M218   2006
  599.64'8—dc22
                                                     2005033306

This edition first published in 2006 by
**Weekly Reader® Books**
An imprint of Gareth Stevens Publishing
1 Reader's Digest Road
Pleasantville, NY  10570-7000  USA

Copyright © 2006 by Weekly Reader® Early Learning Library

Managing editor: Valerie J. Weber
Art direction: Tammy West
Cover design and page layout: Kami Strunsee
Picture research: Diane Laska-Swanke
Translators: Tatiana Acosta and Guillermo Gutiérrez

Picture credits: Cover, © Mike Anich/Visuals Unlimited; pp. 5, 9, 13, 19 © Alan & Sandy Carey;
pp. 7, 21 © Michael H. Francis; pp. 11, 15, 17 © Tom and Pat Leeson

All rights reserved. No part of this book may be reproduced, stored in a retrieval system,
or transmitted in any form or by any means, electronic, mechanical, photocopying, recording,
or otherwise, without the prior written permission of the copyright holder.

Printed in the United States of America

2 3 4 5 6 7 8 9 10 09 08 07

## Note to Educators and Parents

Reading is such an exciting adventure for young children! They are beginning to integrate their oral language skills with written language. To encourage children along the path to early literacy, books must be colorful, engaging, and interesting; they should invite the young reader to explore both the print and the pictures.

*Animals That Live in the Mountains* is a new series designed to help children read about creatures that make their homes in high places. Each book describes a different mountain animal's life cycle, behavior, and habitat.

Each book is specially designed to support the young reader in the reading process. The familiar topics are appealing to young children and invite them to read — and reread — again and again. The full-color photographs and enhanced text further support the student during the reading process.

In addition to serving as wonderful picture books in schools, libraries, homes, and other places where children learn to love reading, these books are specifically intended to be read within an instructional guided reading group. This small group setting allows beginning readers to work with a fluent adult model as they make meaning from the text. After children develop fluency with the text and content, the book can be read independently. Children and adults alike will find these books supportive, engaging, and fun!

— Susan Nations, M.Ed., author, literacy coach,
and consultant in literacy development

## Nota para los maestros y los padres

¡Leer es una aventura tan emocionante para los niños pequeños! A esta edad están comenzando a integrar su manejo del lenguaje oral con el lenguaje escrito. Para animar a los niños en el camino de la lectura incipiente, los libros deben ser coloridos, estimulantes e interesantes; deben invitar a los jóvenes lectores a explorar la letra impresa y las ilustraciones.

*Animales de las montañas* es una nueva colección diseñada para presentar a los jóvenes lectores algunos animales que viven en regiones montañosas. Cada libro explica, en un lenguaje sencillo y fácil de leer, el ciclo de vida, el comportamiento y el hábitat de un animal de las montañas.

Cada libro está especialmente diseñado para ayudar a los jóvenes lectores en el proceso de lectura. Los temas familiares llaman la atención de los niños y los invitan a leer — y releer — una y otra vez. Las fotografías a todo color y el tamaño de la letra ayudan aún más al estudiante en el proceso de lectura.

Además de servir como maravillosos libros ilustrados en escuelas, bibliotecas, hogares y otros lugares donde los niños aprenden a amar la lectura, estos libros han sido especialmente concebidos para ser leídos en un grupo de lectura guiada. Este contexto permite que los lectores incipientes trabajen con un adulto que domina la lectura mientras van determinando el significado del texto. Una vez que los niños dominan el texto y el contenido, el libro puede ser leído de manera independiente. ¡Estos libros les resultarán útiles, estimulantes y divertidos a niños y a adultos por igual!

— Susan Nations, M.Ed., autora/tutora de alfabetización/
consultora de desarrollo de la lectura

A baby mountain goat is called a **kid**. Soon after it is born, a kid can stand. It drinks milk from its mother.

▬ ▬ ▬ ▬ ▬ ▬ ▬ ▬ ▬ ▬ ▬ ▬ ▬ ▬

La cría de la cabra montés recibe el nombre de **cabrito**. El cabrito puede pararse poco después de nacer. Bebe la leche de su madre.

In a few days, a kid starts to eat grass.
For about a month, it drinks milk, too.
It stays with its mother for about a year.

━━━━━━━━━━━━━━━━━━━━━━━━━━

A los pocos días, el cabrito empieza a
comer pasto.  Durante casi un mes,
también bebe leche.  Se queda con la
madre durante un año, más o menos.

Kids push and chase each other. They hop off high rocks. They learn how to climb.

---

Los cabritos se empujan y se persiguen. Brincan de rocas altas. Aprenden a trepar.

Male mountain goats are called **billies**.
Female mountain goats are called
**nannies**. Both nannies and billies
grow horns and beards.

----------------------------------------

Las cabras macho reciben el nombre
de **machos cabríos**. Las hembras son
**cabras**. Tanto las hembras como los
machos tienen cuernos y barba.

Mountain goats eat grasses and plants. They gulp down their food.  Later, they bring it up and chew it again.

■ ■ ■ ■ ■ ■ ■ ■ ■ ■ ■ ■ ■ ■ ■ ■

Las cabras monteses comen pasto y plantas.  Engullen la comida deprisa. Más tarde, la recuperan para masticarla de nuevo.

Mountain goats climb well.  They balance on thin ledges.  They bound down steep cliffs.  Their feet grip rocks and ice.

------------------------------

Las cabras monteses trepan bien. Se mantienen en equilibrio sobre estrechos salientes.  Descienden brincando por empinados desfiladeros. Sus patas se aferran a las rocas y al hielo.

15

Nannies and kids stay in groups called **bands**. An old nanny leads each band. Billies join them in winter.

- - - - - - - - - - - - - - - - - - - -

Las hembras y los cabritos se mueven en grupos llamados **rebaños**. Una hembra vieja lidera cada rebaño. Los machos cabríos se les unen en invierno.

Mountain goats live high in the mountains. The weather is cold up there. Heavy coats help keep them warm in winter.

━ ━ ━ ━ ━ ━ ━ ━ ━ ━ ━ ━ ━ ━ ━ ━ ━

Las cabras monteses viven en lo alto de las montañas. Allí, el clima es frío. Sus densos pelajes las abrigan en invierno.

19

In spring, mountain goats lose their thick coats. They rub on bushes. They rub off their winter fur.

------------------------------

En la primavera, las cabras monteses pierden ese denso pelaje. Se restriegan contra los arbustos. Al restregarse, el pelo invernal se cae.

winter fur/
pelaje de invierno

21

# Glossary

**balance** — to keep steady

**bound** — to jump

**grip** — to hold onto

**gulp** — to swallow a lot quickly

# Glosario

**aferrarse** — sujetarse

**en equilibrio** — sin caerse

**brincar** — saltar

**engullir** — tragar deprisa

# For More Information/Más información

## Books

*Goats.* Animals That Live on the Farm (series).
JoAnn Early Macken (Weekly Reader Early
Learning Library)

*Mountain Goat.* Zoo Animals (series).
Patricia Whitehouse (Heinemann)

## Libros

*La cabra montes/Mountain Goat.* Animales del
zoologico (series). Patricia Whitehouse (Heinemann)

*Goats/Las cabras.* Animals That Live on the Farm/
Animales Que Viven En La Granja (series). JoAnn
Early Macken (Weekly Reader Early Learning Library)

## Web Sites/Páginas web

I'm a Mountain Goat
Yo soy una cabra montés
*www.pbs.org/kratts/world/na/mtgoat*
Mountain goat creature profile from *Kratt's Creatures*
Información sobre las cabras monteses en la página
de *Kratt's Creatures*

# Index

# Índice

## About the Author

**JoAnn Early Macken** is the author of two rhyming picture books, *Sing-Along Song* and *Cats on Judy*, and more than eighty nonfiction books for children. Her poems have appeared in several children's magazines. A graduate of the M.F.A. in Writing for Children and Young Adults Program at Vermont College, she lives in Wisconsin with her husband and their two sons.

## Información sobre la autora

**JoAnn Early Macken** ha escrito dos libros de rimas con ilustraciones, *Sing-Along Song* y *Cats on Judy*, y más de ochenta libros de no ficción para niños. Sus poemas han sido publicados en varias revistas infantiles. JoAnn se graduó en el programa M.F.A de Escritura para Niños y Jóvenes de Vermont College. Vive en Wisconsin con su esposo y sus dos hijos.